Encouraging Words

Jill Sheehan

VERITAS

Published 2006 by
Veritas Publications
7/8 Lower Abbey Street
Dublin 1
Ireland
Email publications@veritas.ie
Website www.veritas.ie

ISBN 1 85390 957 2

Copyright © Jill Sheehan 2006

First published as part of *Intercom* magazine,
published by Veritas Publications

Quotations from Dietrich Bonhoeffer are reproduced courtesy of the
Dietrich Bonhoffer organisation. Quotation from Brother Roger
reproduced with the kind permission of Taizé international. Quotations
from Henri Nouwen taken from *With Open Hands* (Ave Maria Press, 1995)
and *The Inner Voice of Love* (Doubleday, 1996) included with permission.
All quotations from Thomas Merton used with permission of the Merton
Legacy Trust. Quotations by Oscar Romero are taken from *The Violence of
Love: The Pastoral Wisdom of Archbishop Romero* (HarperCollins, 1998)
reproduced with permission.

A catalogue record for this book is available from the British Library.

Designed by Colette Dower
Printed in the Republic of Ireland by Betaprint, Dublin

*Veritas books are printed on paper made from the wood pulp of
managed forests. For every tree felled, at least one tree is planted,
thereby renewing natural resources.*

Introduction

Jill Sheehan's 'Encouraging Words' have appeared in *Intercom* magazine for the past seven years, offering opportunities for reflection for lay and religious readers alike. Whether you are new to Jill's writing or are already familiar with those *Intercom* pieces, this collection provides thoughtful and heartfelt reflections for times of joy and trouble.

As we face the day-to-day challenges that life throws at us, Jill reminds us that a few well-chosen encouraging words can make our journey that little bit easier. She also emphasises the importance of remembering the love that God has for us, of appreciating the blessings we have received, of remembering the word 'Thanks', of being a 'cheerful giver' and of using our hearts for love.

Encouraging Words, with its simple but significant message of optimism and appreciation for what life offers, makes a perfect bedside book and encourages us to act with the courage, charity and kindness needed to fulfil our calling as Christians.

Many years ago a friend told me I should take up writing. His suggestion amazed me. When eventually I put a blank sheet into the typewriter, I could not imagine that I had anything to say that had not already been said better by someone else. I had a fear of expressing what was in my mind and heart. My fears often made me delay or even abandon my writing plans.

Every time I write, I overcome these fears and trust not only my own unique way of being in the world, but also my ability to give words to it. This gives me a deep spiritual satisfaction.

What I am gradually discovering is that in the writing, I come in touch with the Spirit of God within me and experience how I am led to new places. Writing does not come easy but it reveals what is alive in me. To write is to embark on a journey whose final destination we do not know.

Writing requires an act of trust, because we do not yet know what's in our hearts. We hope it will emerge as we write. Once we dare to put on paper the few thoughts that come to us, we start discovering how much is hidden underneath these thoughts and gradually come in contact with our own riches. I owe a deep gratitude to the Lord for this gift.

At the start of each spring, taking 'one day at a time', it's good to reflect on the following, from the pen of an Indian wise man:

> I slept and I dreamed that life was joy.
> I woke and saw that life was but service.
> I served and understood that service was joy.

Christ's apostles weren't able to watch one hour with him. Their intentions were good but the frailties of the body betrayed them and they slept while Jesus endured his agony. Many people have had the same experience that Christ had – nobody seemed available in time of need. But ordinary people, struggling to contend with their own lives, find it particularly hard to make a commitment outside their own concerns.

Those who do so, those who manage to stretch themselves to give help and comfort to others in good times and in bad, transcend their ordinariness. And there is hope for the human race when that Christ-like compassion is visible.

> Compassion is the most beautiful of all God's names.
>
> Victor Hugo

Looking through a calendar produced by the Irish Sisters of Charity for 1999, I was touched by a photo of a smiling little African boy, with a proverb printed under it:

> Happy are those who light fire in the hearts of others.

Since Christmas I got many opportunities to reflect on this saying, as a special friend of mine – a contemplative Sister – was dying. The news of her approaching death was heartbreaking for me. But she was longing to meet the Lord she loved and served so faithfully.

Many years have passed since our time together in the Ursuline Convent in Cork. When she died, I thought to myself: no more phone calls or letters from Sheila. But then I thanked the Lord for the fire she lit in my heart, as we shared our love of Jesus and his message, which was so precious.

Why was Sheila (Sr Jordan) so special in my life? Firstly, because I was conscious that my desire to spread the Word of God was part of her many hours of prayer; secondly, because of her affirmation and joy when the Lord used me to show His love; and lastly because of her sense of humour and deep humanity, and her understanding in difficult moments of life.

I know Sr Jordan will be sadly missed by the sisters in Siena Convent and by all who loved her. Her meeting with Jesus should bring her closer to us all, because her heart was full of love.

> Let us love one another, because the source of love is God.

> From the moment I knew I had a heart I
> gave it to God.
>
> Mary Aikenhead

This saying of Mary Aikenhead's was in my thoughts during the Funeral Mass for Sr Kathleen Murphy (Ursuline, Cork). Unable to be present, I went apart in my home and spent the time in 'prayer of the heart'.

Kathleen and I met on our first day of boarding school, many years ago. She was great company; we prayed, laughed and studied together. Her decision to enter Blackrock came as no surprise because I knew she had given her heart to God and the Ursuline order. Nothing was impossible to her where the love of the Lord and people were concerned as she travelled far and wide spreading the Good News.

During my prayer and in the midst of some tears, my eyes were opened to the truth of myself as well as to the truth of God. How precious we are if only we give our hearts to

God. In spite of, or because of, the purification experienced in the Church, there are people who open their hearts and give them to God in love of Him and his beautiful message for our challenging times.

> Welcoming Christ in the peace of our nights, in the silence of our days, in the beauty of creation, in the hours of intense inner combat, welcoming him means knowing that he will be with us in every situation always.
>
> Br Roger

Yesterday's gone sweet Jesus,
And tomorrow may never be mine,
Lord help me today, show me the way,
One day at a time.

A popular author wrote: 'Yesterday is a cancelled cheque, tomorrow is promised to no one, the only thing you have is *right now*.'

At some stage of life we all spend time reminiscing about the past. It may bring pleasure or pain. Maybe we enjoy our memories and their associations. But we're all products of our past.

While we have negative emotions about our past, it is a wonderful grace if we accept God's love in the present so we are able to look back at life so far and say, 'I can see God's invisible hand in all that I've experienced in my life, both the good and the bad.'

Has the inner pain and turmoil of daily living disappeared? No, but the peace, love, hope and trust in the message of the love of Jesus will ease the ache in our hearts as we live out his teaching 'one day at a time'. Christ can only operate in the present. Our true self, that self which is of God, exists not yesterday, not tomorrow, but only today. Loving God is 'I am', never 'I was' or 'I will be'.

> You show me the path of life,
> in your presence there is fullness of joy;
> in your right hand are pleasures
> for evermore.
>
> Psalm 16:11

13

What does it matter, O Lord, if the future
is dark?
To pray now for tomorrow I am not able.
Keep my heart only for today, give me your
protection today,
grant me your light – just for today.

St Thérèse of Lisieux

Reading this prayer my thoughts turn to the many great, generous women I have met through the years, both religious and lay. They were, and are, caring, compassionate, sensitive and most of all hopeful people.

Naturally religious women are sad at the lack of vocations. While praying in a convent chapel in Dublin some years ago, an elderly nun called me and said, 'Will you pray that this chapel be once again filled with young Sisters?' It never happened. But Sisters with hope, courage and faith in the Lord left their large convents, are living in small communities and ministering to the needs around them.

And what about the committed, dedicated laywomen who are working with the elderly, sick, lonely, homeless and who are alive to the injustices in our world? They bring the words of Thomas Merton to fruition in their lives:

> Unless we learn the meaning of mercy by exercising it towards others, we will never have any real knowledge of what it means to love Christ.

A prayer from Edwina Gateley, who founded the Lay Volunteer Movement:

> My God equally present in darkness as in light, stand by me! Allow me, yes to suffer and be hurt, but not to be broken or destroyed. Allow me to be bruised, but not my spirit to be overcome. I know of suffering and I do not fear it. I only fear my strength to carry it. I ask not to escape from the threat and the pain. I ask that I might carry them.

With grace, with hope, with love.

How important is Jesus in my life? Is he like a star on my horizon, pointing the way to live out his message in daily life. If he is, I must keep connected to the source of all light.

God is like an electrical outlet. Behind every outlet is the mysterious power of electricity. It can light up a room, heat a home and much more. Nothing happens unless we get plugged in, connected to the source of power. And we need the power of God to enlighten our darkness, mend our brokenness, fill our emptiness, enhance our courage and create in us hearts of love.

The connection between all of this is prayer. The psalmist assures us:

The Lord is near to all who call upon him.

There will be times when our star seems covered with dark clouds. Then we can get comfort from that great woman Catherine de Hueck Doherty, who wrote:

Three quarters of your life you will feel as if you cannot pray. Of course you cannot pray as you think you want to pray! Who do you think you are, an angel who can say to God for all eternity: glory, glory, glory?

But God sits there and doesn't mind at all. God prays for you, as you pray about the living, the suffering, the doubting and all manner of things.

God is there, and once God is there, all things are there and you become a prayer.

Do not let your hearts be troubled. Believe in God, believe also in me. In my Father's house there are many dwelling places. If it were not so, would I have told you that I go to prepare a place for you?

John 14:1–2

Faith is our absolute assurance of the divine presence within. At times it protects us from despair and makes life meaningful.

Faith enables us to experience happiness in our relationship with God, especially in our dark moments. Then the rays of light shine through the clouds and trust in God allows us to put aside our hurts and worries, focus on the present moment, give ourselves to others and open our hearts.

We have the powerful words of St Paul that

neither death, nor life, nor angels, nor rulers, nor things present, nor things to come, will be able to separate us from the love of God in Christ Jesus our Lord.

Romans 8:38–9

These words will help to free us from the fear of living and open our hearts to the possibility of loving.

How many times have we had to step out in faith, saying 'I don't know what the outcome is going to be, but I have faith that I'm supposed to be doing this'.

Back in the late 1960s when dialogue and community were the 'in' thing in the church, I offered my services as a secretary to a team offering retreats to mixed groups to encourage the teachings of Vatican II. As a layperson I stepped out in faith to do this work because of my own gift of conviction that the Lord is in the driving seat in all our lives.

> Our soul waits for the Lord; he is our help and shield.
>
> Psalm 33:20

Lent is the time for enjoying God's mercy

It is easy to discourage, and far too easy to
criticise, complain, rebuke. Let us try to be
quicker to see even a small amount of
good in a person and concentrate on that.
Desmond Tutu

A s I reflected on this saying, my thoughts
turned to Ash Wednesday and what I could take
on for Lent.

How much do we appreciate the cry for God's
mercy at the beginning of each Mass? There is
probably no prayer said so frequently and
intimately as 'Lord, have mercy'. It is the cry of
God's people. With God's grace, this cry will
come to fruition in my heart this Lent.

This cry for mercy is only possible when we
are willing to confess that we have something to
do with our failures, accepting our responsibility
even for the pain we didn't cause directly. When
'Lord have mercy' emerges from a contrite heart

(in contrast to a hardened heart) it will not blame but will acknowledge its own part in the sinfulness of the world. It is ready to receive God's mercy.

We choose a life of forgiveness, peace and love, because the Lord we meet on Ash Wednesday and on the road to Calvary is 'the Lord of compassion and love'.

The object of Jesus' command is always the same: to evoke wholehearted faith, to make us love God and our neighbour with all our heart and soul.

Deidrich Bonhoeffer,
The Cost of Discipleship

As Lent begins during the month of February, which means also the arrival of springtime and the start of a six-week period of preparation for the Feast of Easter, we have time not only to appreciate the cost of discipleship, but the unselfish love of Jesus for us all as He went through his agony and death on the Cross. How will we respond to Our Saviour during this spiritual season which calls for greater openness to the word of God and a conversion in every area of our lives? The more we are convinced of God's love for us, and how precious and beautiful this love is, the more capacity we have to love others. The more we reflect on God's love, mercy and forgiveness the more we will be challenged in the way we relate to other people. We can hardly expect to receive God's beneficence and not dispense it to others.

To be loved by God means not only loving him in return, it also means finding the purpose for my own being in that love. From this growing wholeness I can relate to others in ways that are positive, freeing and empowering. Deeply loved by God, therefore, I am empowered to reach out to others.

O Lord, make this Lenten season different from the others. If I have not been faithful in following your way, let me find you again.

'**M**ore things are wrought by prayer than this world dreams of' says Alfred Lord Tennyson. Let us begin the planning of our Lenten resolutions with a positive outlook, taking the advice of St Paul who says, 'God loves a cheerful giver'.

Cheerfulness is characteristic of the real Christian. So let this Lent be not only cheerful but deeply joyous, because we have determined to turn to God. Anyone who turns to God receives an outpouring of his love, is deeply at peace and can be a useful instrument in God's service.

On our pilgrim way we should take to heart a passage written by Pope Paul VI in 1975:

> The world is calling for evangelisers to speak to it of a God whom the evangelists themselves should know and be familiar with as if they could see the invisible.

In other words, with the eyes of faith we have to look beyond the visible things that we can see to contemplate the invisible ones that we cannot see (Romans 1:19). What we need in today's world are experts in humanity, who know the depths of the human heart, who can share the joys and hopes, the agonies and distress of people while remaining contemplatives who have fallen in love with God. All of us are called to be more deeply spiritual.

Prayer is a priority for all of us. People want to hear about God and about a relationship with him. Prayer is that relationship. The people of God on their journey must meet again the pilgrim coming in the opposite direction – the One who is the Way, the Truth and the Life, whom to see is to have seen the Father.

Lent is a time for this, for allowing Christ to be born afresh in our world. And so we pray:

> Lord, give us the strength each day to stand back and dedicate some time solely to you.

Courage comes and goes.
Hold on for the next supply.

Thomas Merton

I t is good to dwell on the importance of expectation, patience and joy in our lives. Jesus not only made us look at our pains but also beyond them:

You are sad now, but I shall see you again and your hearts will be full of joy.

The paradox of expectation is that those who expect joy to come out of sadness can discover the beginnings of a new life in the centre of the old. Those who look forward to the returning Lord can discover him already in their midst.

It can be a precious moment if we realise that we can only expect someone because he has already touched us. God's absence is painful: like our recent winters, it can be weary and sad – and can last for quite a while. However, with trust, we can realise that in the centre of our sadness we can find the first signs of his presence.

Did not the love of the Father for the Prodigal Son grow as he waited for his return home? So also with our intimate relationship with God, present or absent: it can become deeper and more mature while we wait patiently in expectation for his return.

> Let dawn bring news of your faithful love, for I place my trust in you. Show me the road I must travel for you to relieve my heart.
>
> Psalm 14 3:8

How often have we heard the parable of The Prodigal Son? The full value of the message in the parable came alive for me on reading a book entitled *The Return of the Prodigal Son* by Henri Nouwen.

In this book he speaks about the characters of the three people involved, the Prodigal Son, the Elder Brother and finally the Compassionate Father (Henri Nouwen's title).

Giving examples from his own life, he could picture himself in the shoes of all three:

- The return of the Prodigal Son brings hope that God has a 'welcome home' for all of us, no matter how much we stray or turn our backs on him. There will be joy, love and forgiveness waiting for us.
- I always had an understanding for the Elder Son, because he was so human in his reaction to his brother's return. To a certain extent he felt his goodness was not fully appreciated. Jealousy filled his heart; he had worked hard

and the thought must have entered his mind: 'What's going to happen now?'

- Then in the final chapters of the book the author looks on the attitude of the Compassionate Father. As a priest who lived with handicapped people, he felt how much he needed the compassion, kindness, understanding, sensitivity and love of this Father as he dealt with broken, rejected and lonely people in his daily apostolate. Whatever the cost to himself he (Henri Nouwen) knew he had to be there with 'open arms and heart' to welcome those into his family home.

No doubt Jesus welcomed Henri home at the end of his life of love.

Many of us grew up with the wrong ideas about self-love. The impression we got was that to love ourselves was selfish and self-centred, and that self-love took away from love for others. Actually, the more we are able to love ourselves, the more we are able to love others.

As we are aware of the needs of others, we need to be aware of our own needs. When we support and encourage others, we often need to give the same to ourselves. In order to accept others with all their good and bad traits, we have to accept our own faults and failings.

It is often difficult to see the reality of who we are and to encourage ourselves to change, where change is necessary. At the same time we need to compliment ourselves for what is good about us and have the humility to acknowledge and accept the compliments that others give us.

How much do we believe in the unconditional love of God for each one of us? To love ourselves often requires a close relationship with God through prayer. Venturing into solitude with God helps us grow into a deeper acceptance of 'the person God created when He created me'.

It is sad to see the agony of some people who go through life with no self-esteem or self-worth. Life would be less painful if they realised that loving themselves means they become aware of their personal dignity as created beings of God. It means allowing ourselves to experience a sense of worthiness, not for what we do, but simply for who we are.

Loving ourselves means that we come to believe in ourselves and our ability to fulfil the mission of love in the world.

As Jesus rides into Jerusalem on Palm Sunday surrounded by people shouting 'Hosanna', he knows what is ahead of him – an agonising journey of betrayal, torture, crucifixion and death. He is deeply aware of the unspeakable pain to be suffered, yet is strongly determined to do God's will. This is love – far-reaching love – born of an unbreakable intimacy with God, a love reaching out to all people.

Are we, his followers, aware of where we can find strength in a crisis or when facing our cross in life? We have only to contemplate and go apart to a quiet place. Here we will grow in intimacy with Jesus, because there is nobody he does not fully love. In this love we were created. In this love we find mercy.

Peter, having denied the Lord, heard a voice and trusted it. As he allowed that voice to touch his heart, tears came – tears of sorrow and tears of joy, tears of remorse and tears of peace, tears of repentance and tears of gratitude. If we try to love as Jesus loved, we must travel the road of prayer. This helps us to accept the difficulties of daily living. Jesus and his disciples were led to a place where they did not want to go – to the Cross.

On the Feast of the Resurrection let us greet the day with hope. In the words of Henri Nouwen:

> Hope means to keep living amid desperation.
> Hope is knowing that there is love. It is trust in tomorrow.
> In the eyes of another, it is to see that you are understood …
> As long as there is still hope there will also be prayer …
> And you will be held in God's hands.

During the Season of Lent, there are so many messages to reflect on as our thoughts dwell on the sufferings of Christ. His human fear should ease the pain of the sick, lonely and those who feel rejected.

Did not Christ ache for human companionship as he began his agony in Gethsemane? He brought three friends with him and said to them:

> My soul is sorrowful to the point of death. Wait here and keep awake with me.

He didn't ask the disciples to do anything, but simply to be there, because he needed them near him. He cried out to his father, struggling with sadness, fear and loneliness:

> My father, if it is possible let this cup pass me by.

That cry must have helped him, as his great surrendering prayer followed:

Not my will but thine be done.

This suffering in the Garden has inspired many people to heroic patience and love in times of suffering. But it is still part of our human condition to question and complain. We have the desire to escape, find a short-cut or jump over the sickness and pain. Did not the Christ we are contemplating also experience these feelings?

The greatest gift of pardon and tenderness was his act of supreme self-sacrifice from the cross to humanity. This sinful humanity is now welcomed as sons and daughters, as his beloved in whom he is well pleased.

Preparing for the Easter Triduum in heaven

How precious is the Easter Triduum each year in our lives, especially if we reflect on the love of Christ. It is a time to measure our standard of love and compassion as we dwell on our saviour's painful journey to Calvary. The love of Christ was a love without weakness, even in the midst of fear; without selfishness, even in the face of unfair treatment, rejection, mockery. His greatest example on the cross was the ability to forgive.

For three hours he was dying – completely for others. The total exhaustion of his body, the abandonment by his friends, even of God, all became the gift of self. In the midst of dying in complete powerlessness, there was no bitterness, no desire for revenge, no resentment. Nothing to cling to, all to give. How many increased their intimacy with Christ as they travelled the road of Calvary.

My thoughts this year will be with a special friend of Jesus as he travelled that road. Her life was a living witness as she spent so much time in the church going from Station to Station. I was blessed that God sent me such a wonderful friend. And now that Dr Marie is spending her Easter Triduum in heaven, I am filled with gratitude that the Lord was in our friendship up to her death last Christmas, as we offered each other encouragement and love.

We all need an injection of encouragement. So let's reflect on the two downcast disciples on their way to Emmaus. The future looked bleak; their hopes were shattered when Christ was crucified. When the stranger joined them it was good to share their sadness with him.

But he was no stranger – he was someone who lifted their hearts. It was only when he vanished from their sight that their eyes were opened and they recognised who their companion was.

A few questions: What happens to us when Christ seems to have vanished and no longer walks with us? Are we convinced he never refuses his gift of love? Isn't he present when a smile breaks through tears and hope is renewed in the heart of another? Doesn't the most insignificant event speak the language of faith, hope and, above all, love?

In the midst of worries and turmoil, we doubt the sincerity of our prayer, but it is sincere when we can say:

Jesus take me as I am. I can come no other way.

Even with a Christian outlook, the road can seem long, but Jesus keeps us company every step of the way. He will care for you tomorrow as he cares for you today.

How beautiful upon the mountains
are the feet of the messenger
who announces peace,
who brings good news,
who announces salvation,
who says to Zion,
'Your God reigns'.

Isaiah 52:7

I watched the Sunday Liturgy on television on the third Sunday of Easter, from the parish of Borrisoleigh, Co. Tipperary. The liturgy brought home to me the meaning of the above reading by Isaiah because of the sincerity, beauty and riches expressed in the words of the celebrant, the clear readings of the Ministers of the Word, the work of the choir, the chosen hymns and general reverence of the Liturgy. And it certainly brought alive the meeting of the two disciples with Jesus on their sad journey down to Emmaus.

Because of the human touch of the words of the celebrant in his homily I felt very much part of the meeting between Jesus and the depressed disciples. I am sure many viewers' hearts were lifted. A sincere 'thank you' to the parish priest, and all the messengers involved in bringing the 'good news' to our screens that morning.

It is important that we remain open to the God of surprises and his messengers on our road of life, with the help of Thomas Merton's sound advice when he wrote:

> How do you expect to reach your own perfection by leading somebody else's life? His (or her) sanctity will never be yours; you must have the humility to work out your own salvation in a darkness where you are absolutely alone. And so it takes heroic humility to be yourself and to be nobody but the woman, man or artist that God intended you to be.'

On Vocation Sunday, I love to reflect on Jesus' third appearance to his disciples. He asked, 'Simon, Son of John, do you love me?' Peter answered, 'Yes, Lord, you know that I love you.'

When the question was put a third time, Peter was saddened and replied, 'Lord, you know everything, you know that I love you.' In my prayer I pause and thoughts turn to friends, living and deceased, whose lives were a living witness to love for God. I have no doubt that if the Lord put these questions to them, their response would be the same as Peter's.

Then the apostles received a second call to discipleship – no conditions, no rebuke or blame. This is what God's reign is all about: it is not bought or earned. Because of the Lord's unconditional love, we are invited to share in it, lay or cleric: God's love alone is the reason for our Christian vocation. Our world calls for the affirmation of God's love and compassion, in the lives of those we touch.

That's why at the end of the Gospel of John, Jesus asks Peter three times, 'Do you love me?' God is waiting for us to respond. Life gives us endless opportunities.

Let's not forget – 'God loves a cheerful giver'.

When Jesus saw the crowds he felt sorry for them because they were harassed and dejected, like sheep without a shepherd. Then he said: 'The harvest is rich but the labourers are few, so ask the Lord of the harvest to send labourers to his harvest'.

Matthew 9:36–38

How many listening to that gospel feel this is a call to pray for vocations to priesthood and religious life? We appreciate the importance of loving commitment in these vocations – but we are *all* on mission.

This message from Christ could be very fruitful. As we support each other, we keep our eyes on the Prince of Peace. He doesn't cling to his divine power, but touches the lame, crippled and blind. He speaks words of forgiveness and encouragement – and dies alone, rejected and despised. Keep your eyes on him because Jesus is the source of all peace.

Peace is a gift of God, often hidden from the

wise and famous, but revealed to those who feel empty, inarticulate and poor. Peace should enrich our lives when we are conscious of our community around us, even though our mission and gifts may take us on different paths.

He is a God of surprises! In the Christian community we keep the flame of hope alive among us. We take it seriously so that it can become stronger in us.

Have we not heard Christ's advice (also in Matthew's gospel):

Be not afraid!

Mary is our strong and gentle teacher

During the month of May, let us reflect on the gift the Mother of God is to us. Let us ponder on the beauty of her intimate relationship to God.

The Church has often presented her as an ideal of passive, submissive femininity. We should treasure Mary as a model of strength, because in her 'Yes' to God, she pondered his promise, even when it pierced her soul like a sword. What a powerful evocation of what it can mean to be God's chosen.

On my last visit to Lourdes, my only request to Our Lady of Lourdes was that she would give me a great love of her son. I noticed afterwards that his way of life became more precious to me. I learned to use his gifts to spread the Good News, whatever the cost. Mary showed me that 'the Lord had done great things for me'.

We all have our way to Mary's heart. One day at Mass, the celebrant, instead of giving a homily

on Our Lady, sang the hymn 'Gentle Woman'.
The sincerity of his love for Mary touched many
hearts that morning.

> Gentle Mother, Peaceful dove:
> Teach us wisdom, Teach us love.

Do we allow time for listening to the gentle voice that speaks in the silence of our hearts and calls us 'beloved'? Perhaps we are more eager to listen to other louder voices, saying

> Prove that you are relevant, important and especially successful, and then you will earn the love you desire.

That gentle voice calling us 'beloved' comes to us in countless ways. It comes through our parents, friends and people who have crossed our path, making the Lord present in our lives, often with much tenderness. We are encouraged to keep going when we are ready to give up and stimulated to try again when life seems a failure.

The truth is that we are intimately loved, long before people loved or wounded us. That's the truth spoken by the voice that says

> You are my Beloved.

By listening with great attentiveness to that voice of truth, we will discover within ourselves a desire to hear that voice longer and more deeply. Then we can spread the fruits of our love by opening our hearts to show compassion for those whose pain and suffering have clouded the voice of the Beloved in their lives.

Entering into the pain of another can bring its joys, but often heartbreak as well. But then we remember Mary's 'Yes' to becoming the Mother of God. She said,

> I am the handmaid of the Lord, let it be done to me as you have said.

Mary's wonderful example should bring alive our 'Yes' to the call of the Beloved in our lives.

Put the Spirit in charge!

Pentecost is one of the most consoling and encouraging feasts. In sending the Holy Spirit Jesus showed his understanding for the human weakness which made his apostles fearful men as they deserted him in his hour of need. But they were still his beloved disciples, called by name to follow him.

I learned of the importance of the Holy Spirit many years ago. When discussing my life in Christ with a priest friend, his words were few and far between. I remarked on his silence. His reply was, 'There are times when I leave direction to the work of the Holy Spirit in a person's life.'

As time went on, I became more aware of the power of the Holy Spirit leading me into a deeper unity with the compassionate Christ, and to concrete acts of service. In prayer we meet Christ and in him all human suffering. In service we meet people and in them the suffering Christ.

Be perfect, therefore, as your heavenly
Father is perfect.

Matthew 5:48

We would like to be perfect, but we could
become too timid to take risks, which are often
necessary. We must make room for growth to
maturity. When we allow the Holy Spirit to guide
our lives, we will respond to Christ wherever he
reveals himself.

'**Y**ou have good friends in the Holy Souls' said a friend recently. Two of my Holy Soul friends come to mind.

The first is a girl who worked with my mother, looking after us around the time I received First Holy Communion. As Maggie dressed me in all my finery, I was singing some popular song. I have never forgotten Maggie's words: 'Jill, you shouldn't be singing that song on your First Communion morning.' Maggie's gift to me was a deep respect for Christ's gift to me of the Eucharist.

My second memory is of a parish priest in Kanturk who died many years ago. Canon O'Leary was ill for some time before he died, so my brother took him out for a drive on Sundays. John was unable to do so one Sunday, so he asked me to fill in.

I didn't know how the canon would react to my company but I ended up on a tour of the many parishes he ministered in, places I had never seen in our diocese of Cloyne. When we arrived back he thanked me and added, 'God bless you'. The canon was a deeply spiritual man who opened my eyes to the importance of being sensitive to the humanity of all. Remembering him, I ask the Lord to keep me compassionate on my journey of life.

The coming of summer marks the time of the year when many people are changing the direction of their lives. Some are probably helped by the prayer of Dietrich Bonhoeffer in his prison cell:

> Who am I? This or the other? Am I one person today and tomorrow another? Am I both at once? A hypocrite before others, and before myself a contemptibly woebegone weakling? Who am I? They mock me, these lonely questions of mine. Whoever I am, thou knowest, O God, I am thine.

This may be a difficult year for making decisions, but Christ is not waiting in the wings. He does not wait to be invited: ever at work, even when we are not looking for him. He continues to be Lord of life, at work in the Church and the world. He comes: we simply have to make him welcome.

Some people struggle with questions regarding their identity, purpose and life direction. Maybe they think God has forsaken them. But they need not be without consolation, as it will come when they learn to commit themselves into the hands of God, who doesn't give answers, but loves us nonetheless.

How consoling it is to realise that even if I am not sure about who I am and where I am going, I can be sure that God knows my uncertainty and, in his time, will show me the way.

My thoughts this month turn to the Jubilarians of 2001 congratulated by the Editor in the June *Intercom*. No matter what our role in life, time does not stop for anyone. If we realised how much energy is spent holding onto things, then maybe letting go and being alive to people with greater needs would become important in our living.

If you celebrate your Silver or Golden Jubilee this year, are you aware of the retired people who could do with a listening friend to share their memories with? If you are a reader or music lover, don't leave your books or tapes gathering dust while they could be enjoyed by another.

I would like to pay tribute to Fr O'Connell from the Cloyne diocese who died last May. He retired as PP Banteer some years ago and decided to stay on as curate. I remember the day his successor was inducted. The ceremony must have been painful for him. 'Thank you for all your great work down the years,' I said. His face lit up!

We could all do with encouraging words, especially as the years roll by. When we have friends for our journey we are given life to face changes. They continue to challenge, inspire and support us – and help us laugh at ourselves. They call us to greatness on our difficult days.

Do remember with gratitude the good friends the Lord has sent you.

Let there be love and understanding
among us.
Let peace and friendship be our shelter
from life's storms.
Eternal God, help us to walk with good
companions,
to live with hope in our hearts ...
A Jewish Prayer

I appreciate the dedication, commitment and
love shown by women in the service of the
Church. My heart is full of gratitude for those
who never counted the cost of following Jesus. I
was sad to hear of the death of a long-time
friend, Sr Angela Bowe, who was a novice when I
was a boarder with the Ursulines in Cork. She
lived a long life of dedication to God's work.

I have never had any doubts about the value
of the role of women in spreading the good news
through their talents and unselfish work,
whether in lay or religious life. But I wonder how
long more women will be patient to wait for

appreciation and affirmation of their gifts? What kept the women at the foot of the Cross? Let's pray that the Church will wake up to the fact that the love of the crucified is still at work in the lives of women, who also share the gifts of the resurrected Christ.

One of Christ's commands to his followers was 'Love your neighbour as yourself'.

If we are genuine and sincere in responding to this command we have to ask ourselves: 'Do I love myself?' 'How do I love myself?' and maybe the most important question of all, 'Why do I love myself?'

The answers will call for a healthy appreciation of the person created when God created me. They will teach me to be aware of the gifts and talents he blessed me with. And they will deepen the belief that he loves me as I am, because of his tremendous gift of faith to me.

It is consoling to read in the Gospels that what mattered most of all to Jesus on making Peter head of the Church was the reply he received to the question he repeated three times; 'Do you love me?' Like many of us, Peter must have been conscious of his faults and imperfections, but Jesus saw the whole person of the disciple he loved.

I wonder what would be our response if Jesus put this personal question to some of us today: 'Do you love me?' Are we so convinced of his love for us that our response would be a joyful, hopeful and trusting faith by trying to follow in his footsteps?

Jesus, give me a little of your compassion and love as I try to acknowledge by my life that my answer to your question is 'Yes.'

I do love you, but please increase my love.

I have always loved St Peter because of his humanity. He must have blamed himself for his 'short fuse' and for the times he let Jesus down – Jesus whom he deeply loved, a love which was returned a hundredfold.

We all have our faults and failings but we know Christ is with us. I am conscious that growing in my love for him means not only walking in his footsteps but opening my heart with love, compassion, respect and humility in my encounters with others. Remember St Augustine:

> He loves each one of us, as if there were only one of us.

Rules or regulations should not interfere with our kindness, understanding and our listening ear for those in need – whether it is in a parish or family situation, or around the table at bishops' meetings in Maynooth. Let's pray that 'the truth will set us free'.

Jesus had a need of close and intimate friends, those women and men whose touch he needed. One washed his feet and dried them with her hair. These touches helped Jesus continue his mission when his spirits were low.

Let's pray for each other.

> Time is the deposit each one has in the bank of God, and no one knows the balance.
>
> R.W. Sockman

The balance remaining in each of our lives is God's secret. But do we appreciate the value of time spent desiring God's presence in our daily living – however short or long before our deposit is closed?

Let's reflect on the words of Thomas Merton as we wait:

> Man's greatest dignity, his most essential and peculiar power, the most intimate secret of his humanity is his capacity to love. Love is the key to the meaning of life. It is at the same time transformation in Christ and the discovery of Christ. As we grow in love and in unity with those who are loved by Christ (that is all mankind), we become more and more capable of

grasping something of the tremendous reality of Christ in the world, Christ in ourselves and Christ in our fellow man.

In July and August, let's dwell on the influence of St Oliver Plunkett, St Ignatius Loyola and St Maximilian Kolbe. These lovers of Christ are honoured during these months. Through their commitment to Jesus they transformed the lives of many.

We try to follow in their footsteps. We receive and spread God's love in our own lives. And we help to ease the cares and burdens of our fellow travellers on the road of life.

We have never deceived ourselves by pretending to be angels on earth, but we know that Christian perfection and union with God must be realised in the treadmill of this daily life.

Thomas Merton

My spiritual director gave me this valuable message many years ago (in his own words). It was a time when I longed to get closer to God, 'my way'. But my eyes were opened to the importance of my spiritual director's advice – and also to a saying of Gandhi's:

Whatever you do may seem insignificant, but it is most important that you do it.

Over the years, in my daily 'Yes' to God's plan for my life, my increase in faith and love of God has not only depended on my relationship with Jesus, but also on my respect for and appreciation of each person I encounter.

While there may be good as well as difficult days to live through, being aware of the influence of Jesus and his message will bring openness, generosity and the courage to respond to his call.

> God is at home. It is we who have gone
> out for a walk.
>
> Meister Eckhart

Prayer is all about our attitude

No two people walk more than half way
on the same road to God.

St John of the Cross

We can spend a lot of time measuring
our prayer and judging our progress, not
realising the only measuring rod of prayer is love
and our willingness to share that love with
others. Often when our prayer seems poorest in
our own eyes, it may be the most precious in the
eyes of God. In prayer the heart is more
important than the lips, the attitude of mind
speaks louder than the words we use.

Prayer then, is more than words, it is sharing,
sharing your life with God. You discover his love
for you and then you respond. In prayer we
show our appreciation of the importance of
saying 'Yes' to God – even on the rocky miles of
the journey of life.

The sincerity of our prayer is tested when we can turn to Christ in the midst of turmoil and say: 'Jesus, take me as I am, I can come no other way.' Becoming a Christian is a lifelong journey, but it helps to believe that Jesus keeps us company each step of the way.

Our lives are different from the day we discover prayer, not as a last resort, but as a first resort.

> God calls us to be fellow workers with
> him, so that we can extend his Kingdom of
> peace, justice, goodness, compassion and
> caring.
>
> Desmond Tutu

A s people of God, whatever our vocation,
do we try to extend God's kingdom, as Desmond
Tutu suggests? Or are we only interested in the
now famous 'Celtic Tiger', and indifferent to
those who do not benefit from the wealth it
created? And do you, like me, need a break from
the reporting of recent and not-so-recent
scandals – especially the silent attitude of those
who support the *status quo*?

It was a breath of fresh air for me to share a
meal with a priest-friend home from Zambia for
a well-earned rest and listen to him talk of his
work there. Although we see programmes about
the extreme poverty and the terrible sufferings
of AIDS victims and so on, listening and
appreciating the pain of a 'witness' to such

suffering was a moment of self-development for me in following Christ.

It takes courage to be a true witness and to say 'Yes' to Christ, realising that the Christian life is not a way out, but a way *through* life.

> There is no fear in love, but perfect love casts out fear. For fear has to do with punishment, and he who fears is not perfected in love.
>
> 1 John 4:18

There is a very negative attitude about the role of the Church today, with comments like the numbers attending Mass are decreasing all the time. Certainly, it's a changing world, which means if we believe God's love simply adds a bit more warmth and security to our lives, then we are hardly likely to make changes and commitments in our personal lives.

Faith in all our lives will come alive when God's word challenges us to the very core of our being and His Message will result in great commitments and sacrifices in our times. Faith increases when we realise God does not charm us with his grace and love so that we will remain mesmerised by His presence, but so that we will serve Him freely and boldly in our world.

Speaking about faith, Rose Kennedy said in an interview on one occasion:

> I have come to the conclusion that the most important element in human life is faith. If God were to take away all the

blessings, health, physical fitness, wealth, intelligence, and leave me with but one gift, I would ask for faith – for with faith in God, in God's goodness, mercy, love for me, and belief in everlasting life, I believe I could still be happy, trustful, leaving all to God's inscrutable providence.

How true is the following saying in committed people we all have known:

Witness is a silent proclamation of the Good News and a very powerful and effective one.

On the Feast of the Transfiguration, the celebrant at Mass asked us during his homily: 'How important is Jesus in your lives?' Having suggested we think about this, I let the question penetrate my being.

I pondered on the following thoughts:

- In the past, what response have I made to Christ?
- How do I respond to Christ now?
- What response should I make to Christ?

Naturally, what matters is the 'here-and-now' of all our lives, as we try to bear witness to God's message in our world. We will have to convince ourselves that God's love is all-powerful, no matter what doubts assail us.

The more you sense God's call, the more his love will give you an ever clearer vision of your call – as well as of the many attempts to pull you away from it. It will certainly demand a deepening of the knowledge of his love in your heart, and then the fruits of his response will be abundant.

When you know that you are held safe in the love of Jesus (and 'nothing is impossible to him'), your inward journey will open your heart and eyes to the fact (in answer to the celebrant's question) that Jesus is at the core of your being.

> And this is love, that we walk accordingly to his commandments.
>
> 2 John 6

In the morning, long before dawn, he got up and left the house, and went off to a lonely place and prayed there.

I n these words of Jesus, we sense that the secret of his ministry is hidden in that lonely place. There he found courage to follow God's will and not his own, to speak God's words and not his own, to do God's work and not his own. Jesus reminds us constantly:

I can do nothing by myself, my aim is to do not my own will, but the will of him who sent me.

John 5:30

A life without a lonely place (a quiet centre) easily becomes destructive. In those quiet moments of solitude we discover that being is more important than having and that we are worth more than the result of our efforts. We see that life is a gift to be shared. Maybe the healing words we speak are not just our own, but are given to us.

Live your life to the fullest, but don't forget to return to your quiet centre, even in the middle of your actions and concerns, where your concern for others can be motivated more by their needs than your own. Then you can care, then you can give love and hope.

When mystics stay quiet in the muteness of naked truth, attentive to the darkness which baffles them, a subtle and indefinable peace begins to seep into their soul – what is it? It is hard to say, but one feels that it is somehow summed up in the 'will of God' or simply 'God'.

Thomas Merton

A few years before Merton died, he was asked if he would change his books on prayer if he was to rewrite them. His reply was that he would only write one sentence: 'Be still and listen.'

I was a flu victim for many weeks, which drained me mentally, spiritually and physically. But while waiting on the Lord with empty hands, I learned eventually the deep need I had to slow down and listen. I needed to get to know God, not things about God.

It took some weeks before the light came through the clouds, helped no doubt by the prayers of friends. I was moved to listen to some favourite hymns on tapes. Then I found a tape on the spirituality of Thomas Merton. This opened my heart and eyes to the important message coming through to me.

I know as long as I live that the struggle to love God, my neighbour and know myself will still go on. But hopefully I will always keep the words of Teresa of Avila in my heart:

> Believe me, the safest thing is to will only what God wills, for God knows us better than we know ourselves and loves us.

I will call back into my memory the gifts I
have received ...
Stirred to profound gratitude ...
I will consider how all good things and
gifts descend from above ...
Just as the rays come down from the sun,
or the rains from their source.

Ignatius of Loyola
from the 'Spiritual Exercises'

I reflect often on the many gifts I have received
down the years. This helps me appreciate the
influences on my life as a follower of Christ,
which have been a wonderful gift from God. For
example, I have learned from the dedicated
Christian lives of others that I am praying (or
trying to pray) out of my own inner truth, which
helps me live my faith from day to day. Religion
only becomes genuine and sincere when we take
it off the shelf and personalise it.

Gratitude to God is very much part of faith,
especially gratitude to the people in my life, past

and present. Because of their love of God and neighbour, they showed me what life lived with faith, hope and love is all about. What tremendous goodness is all around! How blessed we are by the good example of the beauty of God's action in people's lives!

In the letter to the Hebrews the author tells us that 'faith gives substance to our hopes and makes us certain of realities we do not see'. And how precious is this teaching:

> They who trust in him will understand the truth, those who are faithful will live with him in love, for grace and mercy await those he has chosen.
>
> Wisdom 3:9

While he was in prison in Germany, Dietrich Bonhoeffer wrote: 'I look back on the past without any self-reproach and accept the present in the same spirit'.

How can we face the future with hope and faith if we linger around the 'might-have-beens' of the past?

If I had only done things differently, this way or that, would life have been easier? Who knows? But how true is the saying of A.J. Cronin: 'Worry never robs tomorrow of its sorrows, it only saps today of its strength'.

If our past has been positive, we should be thankful. If it has been negative, we are called to be forgiving. Life must go on.

The past has to be laid to rest so that we can put our energies into the present which will shape our future. In other words, we learn from our mistakes in order to make the past productive for the future.

How fruitful life would be if we followed the advice of a great spiritual writer who wrote:

Allow the Lord, by love and grace, to let you live in this moment, right now. This moment is as perfect as it can be. And God's call, the needs of the world, will make themselves very apparent. Just respond to the need that presents itself right in front of you, today.

And do not forget to be grateful to the Lord 'for the wonder of your being'.

St Augustine wrote:

> We are told in the Psalms, 'Sing to the Lord a new song'. You may reply, 'I do sing to the Lord'. Yes, of course you sing and I can hear you. But make sure that your life sings the same tune as your mouth.

> Sing with your voices.
> Sing with your hearts.
> Sing with your lips.
> Sing with your lives.

> Be yourselves what the words are about! If you live good lives, you yourselves are the songs of new life.

If we need more good advice, we have the wise words of John Wesley:

> Do all the good you can
> By all the means you can

In all the ways you can
In all the places you can
To all the people you can
As long as ever you can.

Finally:

Happiness is a perfume you cannot pour
on others without getting a few drops on
yourself.

Time is full of eternity.
As we use it so shall we be,
Everyday has its opportunities,
Every hour its offer of grace.

H.F. Manning

September has always been an important month for me (a time for stocktaking my life as a Christian). I am not young any more, so as I reflect on the past year, I ask myself many questions.

How did I react to unexpected situations? For instance, when I fell down the stairs, did I believe the Lord was watching over me? (I had no serious injury.) That time spent recovering from bruises and getting mobile again proved an opportunity to spend time 'in the quiet', a valuable time. Perhaps it was God's way of drawing me closer, to a deeper appreciation of the beauty of his message. (Sincere thanks to my neighbours and friends who were there at my hour of need. How precious is the visible sign of a community of love!)

A high point came last May, when I followed (through parish radio) the Redemptorists' Solemn Novena in Newmarket. It brought back many heavenly memories of my life. My gratitude goes to Fr Pat Reynolds and Fr John Riordan, whose convincing message was a welcome gift to me.

I know that 'nothing is impossible to God', so I hope in his plan for me in the year ahead. In spite of 'old age', I will remain faithful and sincere in my 'Yes' to his will, following in his footsteps.

Finally, I quote one line of Fr Liam Lawton's which always touches me:

> I will thank the Lord, deep within my heart.

When you are feeling down, sad or depressed, it is not very helpful to be told by a well-meaning person to count your blessings. The attentive presence of a kindly, sensitive person might be the blessing you need to bring alive the beauty of words of encouragement, gratitude, affection and love.

These blessings do not have to be invented; how open are we to receive them? They can be gentle reminders of that beautiful, strong but hidden voice of the One who calls us by name and welcomes the love of our commitment to a deep relationship.

The problem of modern living is that we are too busy to notice that we are blessed in many ways. We look for affirmation in all the wrong places.

Ours is a world where people find it extremely difficult to stop, listen and pay attention to the needs of others. People also find it hard themselves to be grateful for the gift of love of someone who, as a neighbour in Christ's terms, will cross the road and bring their blessing with them.

If we take to heart how beautiful it is to be blessed ourselves, or to bless others in our journey through life, the following words from the pen of Henri Nouwen will certainly be meaningful for us:

> Be patient. When you feel lonely, stay with your loneliness. Avoid the temptation to let your fearful self run off. Let it teach you its wisdom; let it tell you that you can live instead of just surviving. Gradually you will become one, and you will find that Jesus is living in your heart and offering you all you need.

Let's repeat, with St Augustine: 'You have struck our hearts with your love, and like arrows that stick in the heart, we bear your words within us'.

'Life is what you make it', some people say. But due to circumstances beyond their control, children can grow into adults who are convinced that everyone is having a worthwhile life and doing great good, except themselves.

This can be due to lack of self-esteem, unhappiness in families etc. The result is that instead of seeing how much they have to offer, they question the uselfulness of their lives.

God is love for every child born. For those who feel sad, lonely or depressed because they do not love themselves, Psalm 139:13–14 has some consoling words to lift their hearts:

> For it was you who formed my inward parts; you knit me together in my mother's womb. I praise you, for I am fearfully and wonderfully made. Wonderful are your works; that I know very well.

John Powell adds the following touching words to reflect on:

There is an old Christian tradition that God sends each person into this world with a special message to deliver, with a special song to sing for others, with a special act of love to bestow.
No one else can speak my message or sing my song or offer my act of love. These have been entrusted only to me.

And always remember:

The Lord is close to the brokenhearted.

Take delight in the Lord, and He will
give you the desires of your heart.

Psalm 37:4

Now and again it is good to reflect on the
gifts the Lord has blessed us with, and then ask
ourselves: How have I used these gifts? Maybe I
have gone through life taking them for granted.

Am I humble enough to respond to Jesus with
heartfelt gratitude, thanking him for the wonder
of my being? Do I ask Jesus to open my eyes and
heart to appreciate the wonder of those who
cross my path daily?

To quote the Letter to the Hebrews:

Let brotherly love continue. Be not forgetful
to entertain strangers: for thereby some
have entertained angels unawares.

Hebrews 13:1–2

The Lord has blessed us with gifts of faith, hope
and love. Do we respond by opening our hearts to

those who need compassion, understanding, forgiveness and a shoulder to cry on? No matter what our vocation in life, how can we walk away from those in need and say, 'We love the Lord; our time apart with him is precious'? If we really value our intimacy with Jesus we cannot keep his gifts to us locked away. Surely we have to spread his Good News.

The heart which is on fire with the love of God becomes an enlarged and generous heart:

> I can do all things through him who strengthens me.
>
> Philippians 4:13

> Clothe yourselves with compassion, kindness, humility, meekness and patience. Bear with one another – and forgive each other.
>
> Colossians 3

This teaching from St Paul is important in our Christian living. Our journey through life must be the 'way of the heart'.

We all have gifts and weaknesses, capacities and needs. The heart is the place where we meet others, suffer and rejoice with them. In the words of Jean Vanier: 'The heart is the place of our one-ness with others.'

Maturing in the love of God, putting our trust in Him, we show our concern for each person as a person. With a listening heart we enter true dialogue, whether in a family, parish, community or in work situations.

We must have the humility to forego the need to control others because the free heart frees others. The heart is the core of our being. Filled with compassion, we learn to be more sensitive to others, to their needs, their cries, their inner pain, their tenderness and their gifts of love.

Travelling by the way of the heart will be hurtful and heartbreaking at times. Was it not a painful experience for Jesus and his Mother? Our consolation will come from Psalm 34:18:

> The Lord is near to the broken-hearted,
> and saves the crushed in spirit.

Hope comes from faith and leads to love. It is, in part, a state of expectancy, the looking forward to the fulfilment of God's promises to us ... These will sustain us when the going gets rough, or the way is difficult.

Cardinal Hume

We often wish we could see into the future. We wonder, 'How will next year be for me?' or 'Where will I be five years from now?'

There are no answers to these questions. Mostly we have just enough light to see the next step, what we have to do in the coming hour or the following day. The art of living is to enjoy what we can see and not complain about what remains in the dark.

When we are able to take the next step with the trust that we will have enough light for the step that follows, we can walk through life with joy and be surprised at how far we go. Let us rejoice in the little light we carry and not ask for the great beam that would take all shadows away.

October brings the Feast of St Thérèse. She wrote:

> The smallest flower, the tallest tree.
> They have a job to do for thee.
> To show the world thy majesty,
> O Lord, have you a job for me?

> If you want God to hear your prayers, hear the voice of the poor. If you wish God to anticipate your wants, provide those of the needy without waiting for them to ask you.
>
> St Thomas of Villanova

The important question for all of us is who are the poor and needy in our lives. Are we aware that we may be in a position to hurt or cause pain to others?

When I was on a retreat team some years ago, I met a young Sister who was a retreatant. We got friendly as she had a good sense of humour, but I sensed she was troubled in some way. She chatted with me one evening and taught me a lesson I have never forgotten.

She had buried a sister of hers some months previously and returned from the funeral heartbroken. Hoping to get a kind word of understanding, she approached someone in authority, asking 'May I speak to you for a while?'

The reply was harsh: 'Not now, I must make my Holy Hour.'

She asked me what I thought of this reply. 'I think Jesus would expect me to listen to you,' I said, 'where he would be united with us in a Holy Hour of healing your pain.'

The retreat was in August. I read the death notice of my friend the following Christmas. I was consoled to hear she was a happier person after the retreat.

> Lord, in gratitude for all you have given me, may I be generous to those in need. Show me the way I can express your love for those around me.

Christianity is not a collection of truths to be believed, of laws to be obeyed, or prohibitions. That makes it very distasteful. Christianity is a person, one who loved us so much, one who calls for our love. Christianity is Christ.

Archbishop Oscar Romero

What more important message could we reflect on? We dwell on the life of Christ, remembering his compassion, respect and kindness to those he met. Nobody was unworthy of his immediate attention. If we love, we follow Christ's example, no matter what difficulties cross our path in life.

I hope I will continue to choose the law of love with a heart of love, which Christ's message brought alive. His is a lesson to follow in our homes, communities, parishes etc. How true should be the words of Christ:

Where two or three are gathered, there I am in the midst of them.

We cannot have a law of love if we have no dialogue, respect and consultation. We cannot deny the beauty of Christ's message of love to every woman, man and child: it is a God-given right for us all.

> Kindness, acceptance, respect and time to listen make up the salve that heals our wounds.
>
> A. Quezado

How compassionate am I in my daily living, especially when I meet people who live alone, people who when they close their hall door are alone with their memories and with the need to share the good and bad days with someone who cares?

Will I look on the needs of the lonely with the compassion, kindness and understanding of Jesus as he spread his message of love? Can I dwell on the feelings of Jesus during his agony in the garden, when the picture of his agony hanging in my bedroom is a daily reminder of the pain and heartbreak of the man alone?

No, I cannot pass by the friends of the Lord, because I know what it means 'to taste and see that the Lord is good'.

In the silence of my heart I must honestly ask myself the question,

> Who are the people in my life who mean the most to me?

Is it not the friend who, instead of giving much advice, solutions or cures, chooses rather to share my pain and touch my wounds with a gentle and tender hand:

> the friend who can be silent with me in a
> moment of despair or confusion;
> who can stay with me in an hour of grief
> and bereavement, and especially face with
> me the reality of my powerlessness.
> That is 'the friend' who cares.

What a happier world ours would be if we could sincerely repeat with St Thérèse of Lisieux, 'In the heart of the Church, I will be love'.

Reflect on the following from the pen of an unknown author:

> Kindness is a language which the blind
> can see and the deaf can hear.

A story is told about a little girl who arrived home late from school. Her mother was angry and asked why she was so late. The daughter replied, 'I had to help another girl who was in trouble.' Her mother asked what she had to do, to which her daughter replied, 'I sat down next to her and helped her to cry'.

In our compassion, the value of presence to another person should not be understated. When we sit with people and help them cry, we give hope, maybe in ways we don't even realise.

Presence is one of the best gifts we can offer to others in need. Being present with others means having a willingness to listen, to be open and definitely a willingness to be faithful. Faithfulness is crucial – a rare commodity today.

At times, it is not easy to cry with people who are in pain, depressed, under stress or experiencing a great loss. If the going gets tough, it would be easier not to get involved. But we rely on our deep belief that the very act of caring is worthwhile because it is 'hope' in action.

Genuine faithfulness does not rely on gratefulness or in results. Yet even the human Christ asked, 'Where are the other nine?' Maybe our hearts will become aware that in caring for others, God is, in some mysterious way, caring for us. So let my prayer be: 'Lord, let me remember your gentle faithfulness, so I can be present to others in the way you always are to me.'

Do we ever think of, or pray, the humble prayer of the tax collector, as he stood inside the door of the temple?

Lord be merciful to me a sinner.

This prayer should be constantly on our lips and in our heart.

We are living in an age where the characters of people are no longer private whether during their time on this earth or when they are deceased. At least in past times, any good deeds were reserved for a topic of conversation during the days of mourning.

It is a consoling thought that Jesus will be our judge, because his message calls the proud to repent and assures those who despair of a new hope.

Thomas à Kempis gives us food for thought in the following saying:

You are not the better because you are praised, or the worse because you are blamed, for as you are, you are, and whatever is said of you, you are not better than Almighty God, the Searcher of your heart, will testify that you are.

Happy the people the Lord has chosen as his own.

Growing up, I always thought the month of the Holy Souls was a dreary month. Not only did the coming of November mean that winter had arrived, but death was a subject I didn't like to dwell on. But as the years passed by and I lost my parents, near relatives and many precious friends, the blessings I received through them leave no doubt in my heart. And the beauty of their example encourages me in my personal encounter with Christ.

I have really begun to pray, praying not with lips or intellect or imagination, but praying out of the very roots of my life, my being. Because of the visible, good lives of my Holy Souls, my encounter with Christ continues to be an occasion to celebrate the place of Christ in my own life.

A prayer of Thomas Merton's means much to me:

> His eyes, which are the eyes of Truth, are fixed upon my heart.

Where his glance falls; there is peace;
for the light of his face, which is the Truth,
produces truth wherever it shines.
There is too joy:
And he says to those He loves – 'I will fix
my eyes upon thee'.
His eyes are always on us in choir and
everywhere and in all times.
No grace comes to us from heaven except
He looks upon our hearts.
And what is more – He looks at us from
within our hearts, for we and He are one.

This Christ who enters our hearts is someone we
come to know as a friend. During this November,
he will draw us closer to our friends, the Holy
Souls, who shared their love and hope during
their lives on earth.

It is really only one simple little truth which I have to communicate: how to begin to live with one's hand in the hand of the Lord.

These are words of St Edith Stein, who held the hands of those she loved as they went to die in the gas chambers.

As I travelled the 'Road of Life', I have been blessed through working with priests, either in a retreat situation or parochial clergy. They made me conscious of the beauty of the gift of priesthood to us all – as we struggle to live 'with our hands in the hand of the Lord'.

Priests are human as Peter was. Fortunately, many know when to listen and when to speak. Once a mutual trust is present we can be silent together and let the Lord speak gently and softly. His presence will continue to bear many fruits in the future. A caring silence can enter deeper into our memory than many caring words.

Both priests and those who expect the Word of God from them should reflect on another saying of St Edith:

> Divine life is love, ever-flowing, unforced, self-giving love which humbles itself compassionately for every creature in need.

Most of those I knew as priests (thankfully not all!) are now Holy Souls. This November I will remember them and what 'Good News' they brought. In the words of St Edith:

> Faith in the Crucified – living faith accompanied by loving dedication – is for us the doorway to life and the beginning of future glory.

What is the relationship between tenderness and faith? We have many examples of tenderness in the life of Jesus, especially to those who needed his healing touch. People approached him without fear of rejection, with complete trust in his tenderness.

Jesus was saddened at the Pharisees' hardness of heart. He looked on them with indignation. Sadly, we have many examples of a lack of tenderness in our world that brings cruelty, sadness and misery to the lives of innocent people. However, we witness deep tenderness when people give their lives and hearts to ease the hunger and suffering in their near and far-away neighbours.

Loving God and neighbour with tenderness involves the courage to take small steps. We must make small affective investments (a smile, a word, a good wish, an expression of thanks). There is wisdom in these small gestures, but we need prudence and courage because we are never certain how we will be received.

Keeping the tenderness of Jesus and his mother before us, we will nourish a constant attitude of tenderness on our road of life.

Quiet time is encouraged – when we
realise, deep in our hearts,
that these precious periods in life help us.
Robert Wicks

What more suitable time than Advent for
me to take advantage of my 'quiet place'? There I
learn what needs attention to make me a better
person. I am glad of this place, where my inner
self will find silence and solitude.

I put great emphasis on quiet time, because I
believe everything begins at home: I must begin
with myself. In this space, I try not to judge
harshly. I avoid panicking or trying immediately
to solve a problem.

Through this quiet time, habits loosen their
hold, so we see life differently (including
ourselves). This quiet time is especially valuable
in Advent as we prepare for the coming of Jesus.

Quiet time keeps us in touch with the Lord
who loves us. For some people this blessing
comes in the fact that they no longer feel

useless. The joy of the Lord fills their hearts because the truth has set them free. The Spirit does wonderful things in and through them.

To pray is to move to the centre of all life and all love.

Henri Nouwen

Enjoy all the comforts of friendship
for they come from God.

Mary Aikenhead

One of the greatest blessings for me has been the gift of precious friends. They are at my side when they see the brightness of a smile, but they also accept my dark days. Because of their sincerity and sensitivity, friends lift my spirits, showing me that 'every cloud has a silver lining'.

For instance, one said to me in a difficult moment, when the Lord seemed to be 'missing': 'Don't worry – I will carry you in the meantime.' That friend's prayer helped me to realise the importance of another saying of Mary Aikenhead's: 'Prayer is never offered without effect.'

Even what some people would call 'Christmas card friends' are precious. This was brought home to me last Christmas week while preparing my list. I got a phonecall from the husband of a friend, a friend I hadn't met for twenty years, since we shared a hospital room. Our only contact since then had been at Christmas. It was with sadness I learned that my cheerful friend Florrie had been buried that day. Offering my sympathy and passing the remark, 'I was very fond of Florrie', her husband's answer was, 'She was very fond of you'.

I hope and trust in the Lord that this year my call to love will be deeper and stronger – so that (in the words of Dorothy Day) my motto will be:

> To love with understanding and without understanding. To love blindly and to folly. To see only what is lovable. To think only on these things. To see the best in everyone around, their virtues rather than their faults. To see Christ in them.

> Serve God with a great heart and a willing mind.

Mary Aikenhead

How important it is to be a 'waiting person', especially during the weeks of Advent! If we have the gift of patience and know what it means to stay where we are and live our situation out to the full, living actively in the present with hope and expectation, we can look forward with joy to the coming of the Child Jesus.

Waiting can be a precious time of learning. The longer we wait, the more we learn about him for whom we are waiting. As the Advent weeks progress, we hear more and more about the beauty and splendour of the One who is to come. The gospel passages read during Mass all speak of events before his birth and of people ready to receive him. Preparing my own welcome, with my 'quiet time' in his presence, leads to a deep inner stillness and joy. I realise that the One for whom I am waiting has already arrived and that he speaks to me in the silence of my heart. This Jesus can be born in my life slowly and steadily, as the one I learned to know while waiting.

Where is God? God is where we are – weak, vulnerable, small and dependent. God is where the poor are, where we find the hungry, the handicapped, the mentally ill, the elderly, the powerless. I realise that I can be God's messenger by staying close to the small, weak, vulnerable child that is within. The Christ-child is within us. Discovering it gives us reason to truly rejoice!

December is a good time to pause and look back on where we have been, notice how far we have come and refresh our dreams and hopes. In January we set out once more.

For many years it has not been possible for me to have a retreat. But I make my birthday in September a special day. This year I spent some hours in silent prayer and reflection under the direction of a priest friend in the Friary in Killarney. I looked on the year just ended and reflected on how I responded to its ups and downs, how I valued the influence of the Lord in bright moments and dark days – finishing with Reconciliation and the Eucharist.

Working on a retreat team for many years I always valued the graces I received in a retreat. I was content at the end of the week if only one retreatant went home renewed.

In the past, people in parishes were aware that in June their clergy went off on their yearly weeklong retreat. Why was this changed to a two-day or three-day retreat? We laity are losing out as well. There is a scarcity of retreats or missions in parishes. Attendance at these may be smaller but the Lord is still touching hearts.

> He leads me beside still waters; he restores my soul.
>
> Psalm 23:2

When you feel the anguished desire for God to come near because you don't feel God present, then God is very close to your anguish. It is then that prayer and religion have most merit; when one is faithful in spite of not feeling God's presence.

Archbishop Oscar Romero

It is good to ponder on these words of such a committed follower of Christ, a commitment which demanded justice for the poor and needy. He put his life in danger and paid the price, as he was shot at the altar as he celebrated Mass.

While there have been many people who have given their lives like Oscar Romero, there are other ways of dying for Christ. We have a great need in our world for people who are a living witness to the Lord's love to all they meet.

What is the mature sign we need in our church? Is it not people (of whatever vocation) who, because of their love, want to live humbly for the cause they believe in? We need people like Blessed Pope John XXIII who, because of his joy, love, empathy and humanity, brought happiness and hope to people.

Where is the joy in our following of Christ today? With the lack of vocations to the priesthood and religious life, maybe we have lost sight of his love. Yet he works wonders no less today than in the days with his disciples.

With hope in the child born in the crib and those around us, let us say with all our hearts:

> You are the Christ, the Son of the living God.

Your true identity is as a child of God.

Henri Nouwen,
The Inner Voice of Love

Visiting the crib at Christmas is a very special part of the beauty of the feast, which parents and children make a family occasion. Jesus' life began in that little stable, surrounded by the warmth of the living animals, the scent of hay and the gentle touch of his mother.

He came into a life of the senses, a life of joy and pain. He walked the dusty roads, drank sweet wine at weddings and laughed and grieved with his friends. He left us an example of a life overflowing with love, hope and compassion, a life brutally ended by those who did not accept this message.

Through it all God sustained him and in the words of St Ignatius, 'Jesus did it all for you and me'. Ignatius tells us to taste with love that heavenly plan, that holy family, to taste Jesus' life. For in that life exists *all* our lives, the essence and vitality of both body and spirit.

Ours is an incarnate faith. The blessings and sorrows of body and soul fill our lives as we enter January. If you have any doubts about the God of love and forgiveness, reflect on the qualities of the friend who was the rock upon which Jesus built his church.

Peter loved and trusted Jesus, but there were times when he didn't understand his mission, even denied him three times. To be welcomed back with the words: 'Do you love me?' – what a lesson in forgiveness and self-acceptance. Having visited the Holy Family at the crib, with renewed faith, hope and love, say from your heart to Jesus in the New Year: 'You know I love you'.

Christ has no body now but yours –
No hands, no feet on earth but yours.
Yours are the only eyes with which
His compassion can look out on a troubled
world.
Yours are the only feet with which
He can go about doing good.
Yours are the only hands with which
He can bring his blessing to his people.
Christ has no body now on earth but
yours

Teresa of Avila

As we reflect on the sufferings, agony and
anguish of Jesus during his passion, we
remember the thousands of people who
suffered and died in the tsunami disaster areas
of South-East Asia and in the South Asia
earthquake. Our prayer of gratitude is for all
who brought alive in these days the words of
Teresa of Avila, as they responded with

generosity to the appeals for help, easing the burdens of those they have never met, brightening their future.